DRAGONBALL Z ®

BY MARIA B. ALFANO

HOW TO DRAW
CHALLENGE
ARENA

SCHOLASTIC INC.

New York   Toronto   London   Auckland   Sydney
Mexico City   New Delhi   Hong Kong   Buenos Aires

ISBN 0-439-56632-0

12 11 10 9 8 7 6 5 4 3 2 1   3 4 5 6 7 8/0

Printed in the U.S.A.
First printing, September 2003

STEP INTO THE DRAGONBALL Z CHALLENGE ARENA

Your challenge: to create action-packed scenes in which the universe's greatest heroes face off against its most evil villains. Will evil triumph, or will the Super Saiyan warriors save the day? The fate of the universe is yours to decide.

In the DBZ Challenge Arena, you choose the characters. You create the battle. You pick the winner!

You'll need:
- sharp pencils
- blank paper
- a good eraser

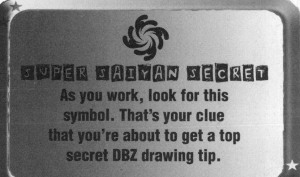

SUPER SAIYAN SECRET
As you work, look for this symbol. That's your clue that you're about to get a top secret DBZ drawing tip.

You may also want:
- a pile of scrap paper
- a thin black marker
- color pencils, crayons, or water-based paints
- a giant bag of gumdrops to keep Majin Buu busy while you work.

Now fire up your Super Saiyan skills and get ready for the ultimate DBZ drawing challenge!

GET IN SHAPE

The DBZ heroes and villains may look hard to draw, but each character starts out with simple shapes like circles, ovals, squares, rectangles, and triangles. Warm up by drawing these basic shapes on a piece of scrap paper. Don't worry about making mistakes. Go fast and be loose. This is just the warm-up. Try not to spend more than five seconds on any shape.

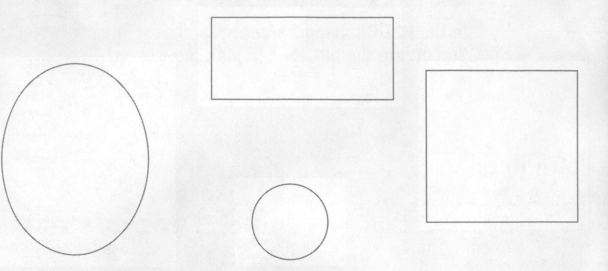

Now that you're warmed up, here are a couple of things to keep in mind before you take on Super Buu and save the universe!

- **Stay Loose**
  For the first few steps in every figure, stay loose and keep your lines light so you can draw over them. Don't think everything you draw has to be perfect.

- **Break It Down**
  Details like eyes, hands, and mouths may seem harder than a battle with Babidi, but these parts are all made of the same basic shapes. Take a look:

HANDS

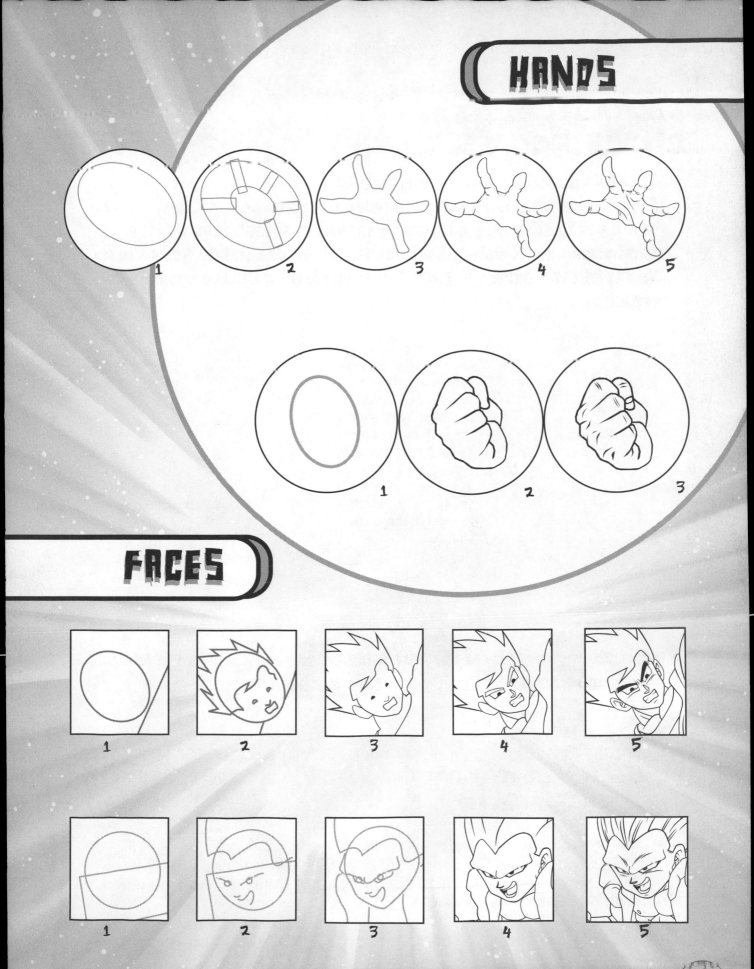

1 2 3 4 5

1 2 3

FACES

1 2 3 4 5

1 2 3 4 5

5

SUPER SAIYAN 3 GOKU®

Super Saiyan 3 Goku is the most powerful warrior on Earth, so you'll get to draw him twice. He's honest, peaceful, loyal, trustworthy, good-natured, brave . . . you get the point. When the safety of the universe is threatened, you'll want Goku on your team!

1 Remember, every drawing begins with simple shapes. Start with a rectangle for Goku's torso. Then draw a circle for his arm in the upper right-hand corner of the rectangle. When you're ready, sketch in the rest of the basic shapes.

SUPER SAIYAN SECRET NEVER FORGET!
Remember, Steps 1 and 2 are about being fast and loose. Use quick, light lines!

2 Connect the shapes with a light, loose line. Take a step back. You already have Super Saiyan 3 Goku's outline on paper.

3

Next, carefully redraw the outline right over the old lines. No erasing yet! Correct the shapes. Check angles and curves.

In Super Saiyan 3 mode, Earth's greatest warrior becomes superpowerful. He can do more damage to his enemies than ever before. Super Buu, beware!

TALK TO THE HAND!
Super Saiyan 3 Goku's hand is bigger than his head in this pose because it's in your face!

5

Finish by adding details. Look closely at the clothes and the extra lines in the hair and outstretched hand. If you like, go over your lines with a marker or darker pencil to make them final. This character is ready to blast into action!

4

Now is the time to erase the lines you don't need. You've already got the shapes and outline, so start adding details like those in the hair and eyes.

CHALLENGE ARENA
Why not draw Goku using his Super Saiyan 3 powers? He can fly, shoot energy beams out of his hands, and move superfast!

SUPER SAIYAN 3 GOKU®

Ready for a challenge? Tackle Super Saiyan 3 Goku's fists of steel!

1

Break Goku's body down into basic shapes. Then draw a big sweeping curve around his head for the hair.

2

Connect all the shapes with a long, curving outline. Erase any distracting lines from Step 1 and decide where you want to place the eyes, nose, and mouth.

COLOR EXPLOSION
The air surrounding Goku takes on an electrical sizzle in Super Saiyan 3 mode. Can you feel it? The energy aura turns his hair blond and his eyes green. Get out those color pencils!

3

Redraw the outline, making sure you've got the curves and angles right. Check the proportions: The face should be about the same size as the fists. In this pose, both feet are the same size.

SUPER SAIYAN SECRET
Always start your drawing with the shape for the torso. Then attach the rest of the basic shapes to that first shape.

It's time to darken the lines and start adding details. In his Super Saiyan 3 form, Goku's hair has a lot of spikes. And don't forget those bulging muscles — start drawing them, using curved lines!

Super Saiyan 3 Goku can communicate using telepathy. (He doesn't even have to move his lips!)

Goku's powerful attacks include SPIRIT BOMB. It's a superhuge attack that draws energy from all living things!

CHALLENGE ARENA

Now that you can draw Goku in his most powerful form, flip to page 30 and draw Super Saiyan 3 Goku facing off against the ballistic pink terror, Majin Buu.

You're in the home stretch. Add more details. Draw short, quick lines on Goku's clothes to show how dirty he gets from fighting evil!

SUPER SAIYAN VEGETA®

In this stance, Vegeta is ready to face any challenge the universe brings. Your mission is to prove you can draw at Super Saiyan level. Bring it on!

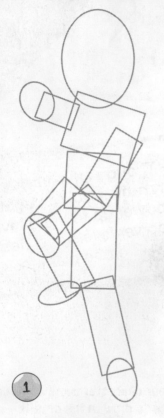

SUPER SAIYAN SECRET
Super Saiyan Vegeta's entire face fits in the bottom third of his head.

1 Start by laying out the basic shapes. The rectangles that will become Vegeta's left arm are drawn *over* and *across* the shapes for his torso and legs. The shapes for his right arm fall *behind* his chest.

SUPER SAIYAN SECRET
Remember to start loose and light — you're going to draw over this first step two or three times before your drawing is done. And keep that eraser locked away until Step 3!

2 Now, using the shapes as a guide, quickly and loosely draw Super Saiyan Vegeta's outline. Then decide where to place his face and lay in that spiky hair! Here's a hint: It's shaped like flames!

Just like Super Saiyan 3 Goku, Vegeta's hair and eye color change when he transforms into a Super Saiyan. His hair is blond, and his eyes are green. So keep those color pencils handy.

Though smaller than his arch-rival Goku, Vegeta can power up to unbelievable power levels and destroy entire planets.

4

Give your character some *character*! It's time to draw in the details — from the flames in the hair to the wrinkle between the eyebrows.

3

Take some time to check the shape of the arms, legs, chest, and head. Make sure everything is the right size. Then erase any lines you don't need. If you like, trace over the final lines with a marker or darker pencil.

MYSTIC GOHAN®

Kick it up! Mystic Gohan is idealistic, good, and pure, just like his father, Goku. When Earth is threatened, Mystic Gohan's true potential is revealed — and it's a knockout! Mystic Gohan is part Saiyan, part human, so he's stronger than either one alone. For this drawing, pretend you are Mystic Gohan's worst enemy (Ew! You're Majin Buu!), and draw this kick coming right at you!

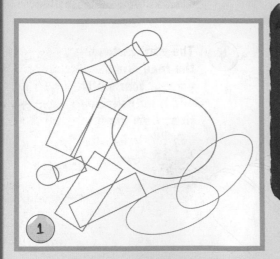

TAKE NOTE:
You're using three big circles for the left leg and foot in this drawing. The shapes are bigger because they are closer to you. They also overlap each other.

In this kicking pose, Mystic Gohan's torso is tilted. Start by drawing the rectangles for his shoulders and stomach on an angle. If you tilt the shapes, you won't have to worry about getting the right angle for the rest of the drawing.

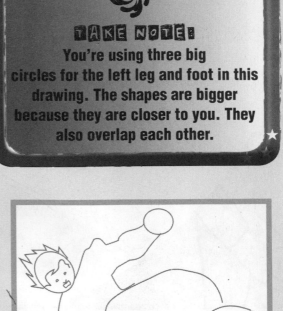

Now connect the shapes with a light, loose line. Don't lose the overlapping — it helps make this drawing look 3–D. The torso stays small. The legs and foot stay big.

WIMP OR WARRIOR?
Although Mystic Gohan starts out as a wimp, his training in the wilderness and his battles against evil transform him into a brave and loyal warrior. Loyal to the good side, that is.

3. Carefully redraw the lines you drew in Step 2 with more accurate lines. Draw on top of what you already have. (That's why you're using a pencil!) Take some time to get the shape of the arms and chest right and to make sure everything is the correct size.

4. The hard part is over! Add details to the face, arms, and clothes. Then go over your outline with a marker or darker pencil and erase any extra lines from the first three steps.

5. This step is all about details. If you get stuck on Gohan's draping clothing, practice on scrap paper first.

13

SUPER SAIYAN GOHAN® IN KAI SUIT

Gohan is a powerhouse! Use your power to conquer this drawing of Gohan gripping the Legendary Z Sword.

1 Start with a tilted rectangle for this Super Saiyan's shoulders. The rest of the body will form a large X. Then draw a long, thin rectangle for his sword.

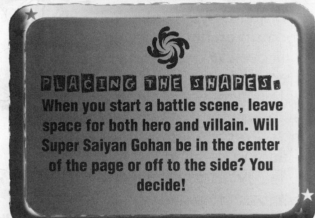

PLACING THE SHAPES:
When you start a battle scene, leave space for both hero and villain. Will Super Saiyan Gohan be in the center of the page or off to the side? You decide!

2 With the speed of a Super Saiyan, connect the shapes with a light pencil line. Place the facial features. Then quickly lay in the outline of Super Saiyan Gohan's clothes and boots. Don't forget the point on that sword!

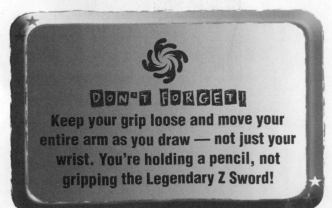

DON'T FORGET!
Keep your grip loose and move your entire arm as you draw — not just your wrist. You're holding a pencil, not gripping the Legendary Z Sword!

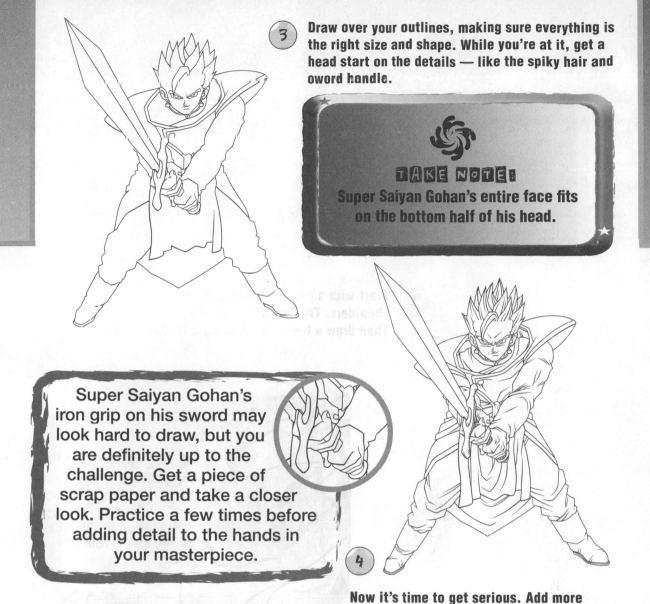

3 Draw over your outlines, making sure everything is the right size and shape. While you're at it, get a head start on the details — like the spiky hair and sword handle.

TAKE NOTE:
Super Saiyan Gohan's entire face fits on the bottom half of his head.

Super Saiyan Gohan's iron grip on his sword may look hard to draw, but you are definitely up to the challenge. Get a piece of scrap paper and take a closer look. Practice a few times before adding detail to the hands in your masterpiece.

4 Now it's time to get serious. Add more details and refine your drawing. Pay close attention to the hands and the shoulder girdle. This is an important part of Super Saiyan Gohan's costume.

CHALLENGE ARENA
Will Super Saiyan Gohan's newly awakened powers be enough to turn the tables on Majin Buu? You decide. Use the background on page 30 and the drawing of Majin Buu on page 18 to challenge the forces of evil in your artwork.

SUPER SAIYAN 3 GOTENKS™

What do you get when you cross Goten with Trunks? GOTENKS! What happens when you infuse him with Super Saiyan powers? You've got a Super Saiyan 3 warrior ready to stand up to Super Buu.

1 Sketch the basic shapes of Gotenks' body. He is squatting, so the rectangles for Gotenks' legs should tilt away from each other.

2 You know the drill! Use light, loose lines to quickly connect the shapes. Draw a big swish around the head for Gotenks' hair. Remember Super Saiyan 3 hair comes down to the waist.

3 Now carefully redraw the outline right on top of the lines you drew in Step 2. Correct the lines as you go along. Check the curves, angles, and proportions.

GET FUSED
When two powerful warriors of equal size and strength combine into one kick-butt superpowerful force, that's fusion! The warriors must train diligently in order to fuse, but once they have mastered the technique, their potential power defies imagination!

(4) Draw over the outline with a black marker or darker pencil. Add details as you go. Remember, in a character's Super Saiyan form, his eyes get narrower, and his hair gets longer and spikier. When you're done, erase any lines you don't need

GOTENKS' SUPERSKILLS
Like Goten and Trunks, Gotenks has the amazing ability to learn moves quickly. He manages to go to Super Saiyan and even Super Saiyan 3 after watching Goku do it just once. Now that's Super Saiyan 3 speed!

(5) Details! Details! Details! Super Saiyan 3 Gotenks has a ton of mighty muscles on his chest. Draw them with curved lines.

SCRAP PAPER POWER
Keep some scrap paper handy to practice the hard parts — like hands and faces — before you try to draw them on your DBZ character.

CHALLENGE ARENA
Now that you can draw Gotenks, try drawing him in this pose. Then flip to page 30 and draw Gotenks challenging Majin Buu inside the Hyperbolic Time Chamber. Who will win? Who will make it out alive?

MAJIN BUU™

Don't mess with Majin Buu! He's much feared and for good reason. Buu can turn his enemies into chocolate or even pink gumdrops. And he uses his tremendous energy to destroy entire planets! The good guys may have their work cut out for them when it comes to taking down Majin Buu, but you already have the skills to do this drawing! Go to it!

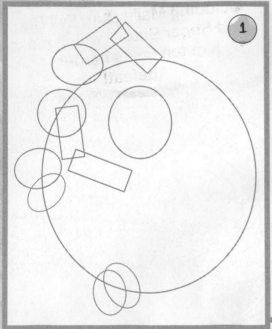

1 Majin Buu is short and round, so you'll use lots of circles and curved lines in this drawing. Start with one big circle. Most of the other shapes you'll need to set up your drawing fit into the upper left-hand quarter of this circle.

TIME OUT!
Take a minute to practice drawing circles on scrap paper. Believe it or not, the faster you draw each circle, the easier it will be to make it round.

Connect the shapes. Add the sweeping swish of Majin Buu's cape and decide where to put the facial features. Buu's gritty scowl begins with a simple rectangle beneath two small curves.

2

THE LOW-DOWN:
Hobbies:
Destroying entire planets.
Current goal:
Destroying Earth.

3 Define your line. Take a minute to look at Majin Buu's hands — he's wearing boxing gloves. Then, draw the outlines of his vest, shirt, pants, and gloves. Begin adding details like Majin Buu's gritted teeth and the flip of his cape.

BUU WHO?
Every good guy in the universe has the same mission: to destroy Buu in all his changing forms! Buu has many forms — including Majin Buu, Evil Buu, and Super Buu — which make him ten times harder to defeat!

Finish by erasing any lines you **4** don't need. Then add the final touches, like the draping of his cape and pants and the squinting lines around his eyes.

Buu doesn't really understand the difference between good and bad. He agrees to stop hurting people when he figures out it bothers Hercule and his puppy, Bee. But when someone messes with his puppy, watch out!

CHALLENGE ARENA
BLOW HIS TOP!
Now that you can draw both Buu and Gotenks, try drawing them in a battle for the safety of the universe. If Gotenks can't get the job done, will Gohan be ready to step up and finish the fight? Just don't get caught in the crossfire!

19

EVIL BUU ™

You wouldn't like Buu when he's angry. Tall and gray, with boxing gloves, Evil Buu is the manifestation of all of Buu's anger. But don't lose your cool. The drawing of Evil Buu is easier to conquer than the character.

1 Evil Buu is facing to the left, so place him on the right side of the paper. Leave enough space to his left for a brave Z warrior. Start with a tilting rectangle for Evil Buu's chest. His head is thinner than the other characters' in this book, so place a thin oval on top of the rectangle instead of a circle.

SIZE IT UP!
Evil Buu is taller and thinner than Majin Buu. While Majin Buu is pink, Evil Buu is gray. They both have rubbery bodies and wear golden boxing gloves — and they are both the biggest threats the universe has ever seen!

Quickly draw the outline of the body, remembering to add the basic shape of Evil Buu's big flowing cape. Place his sinister eyes in the middle of the head. Evil Buu's hands are going to be fists inside boxing gloves, so start out with simple circles. Don't forget the curve on top of his head! **2**

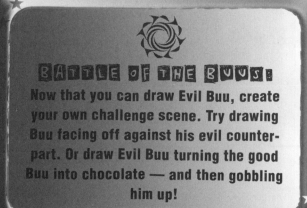

FACE OFF . . . AGAINST THE PAPER!
Staring at a blank sheet of paper can be the hardest part of getting started. That's why it's good to start with light pencil lines. You won't worry about messing up because you can easily erase!

3 Redraw the outline on top of the lines you drew in Step 2. Correct the size and shape of each part. Then carefully go over the outline in darker pencil or marker. Erase any lines you don't need.

4

Now is your chance to be creative! Add the final details and finishing touches. Darken in the belt, vest, socks, and eyes. Then draw the M on his belt and you're done! Evil Buu looks nastier than ever!

BATTLE OF THE BUUS!
Now that you can draw Evil Buu, create your own challenge scene. Try drawing Buu facing off against his evil counterpart. Or draw Evil Buu turning the good Buu into chocolate — and then gobbling him up!

SUPER BUU™

Buu is only Evil Buu for a short time. It's not long before he transforms into a new incarnation of evil — Super Buu! Super Buu is more defined and muscular than Majin Buu, but like all Buus he is rubbery. His powers are awesome — which causes major problems for the forces of good.

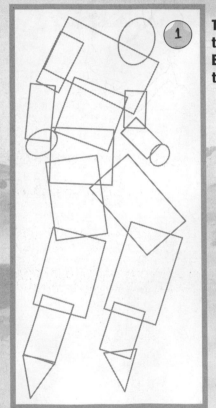

1

This drawing begins with a few more shapes than usual because Super Buu is super tall. But the basic setup is the same. Super Buu's toes are pointed, so use triangles for the feet.

Sketch the outline and add the huge, curving head tail sticking out of the back of Super Buu's head. Remember to use very light pencil lines.

2

Among Super Buu's many new powers is the ability to sense energy levels. With this ability, Super Buu can find Kami's Lookout and go there to fight. Once there, Super Buu launches the most powerful attack ever and causes widespread destruction!

TAKE A CLOSER LOOK:

Super Buu's wrath is great. Take a look at that screaming mouth! Practice tracing Super Buu's face on scrap paper before you draw it on your masterpiece.

③ Now go over your lines and make any adjustments you need. Make sure every part of Super Buu is the right size and shape. Erase any lines you don't need.

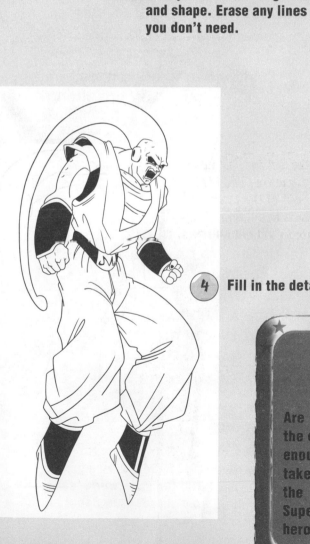

④ Fill in the details before Super Buu attacks!

CHALLENGE ARENA

Are you ready to create the challenge of the century? What brave Z fighter is strong enough, fast enough, and smart enough to take on the worst villain in the history of the universe? The choice is yours! Draw Super Buu facing off against your favorite hero in the Challenge Arena on page 30!

Look out! Dabura is on the scene. As the ruler of the underworld, he's been around for thousands of years. The DBZ warriors can't even count the number of evil acts Dabura has performed in that time. Are you ready to take him on? Warning: This is the most complicated drawing in the book, but you're ready to tackle this tyrant!

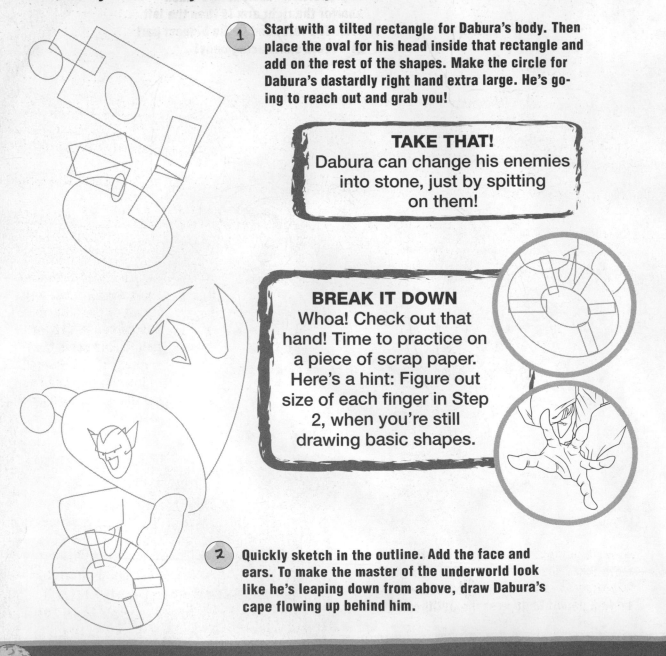

1 Start with a tilted rectangle for Dabura's body. Then place the oval for his head inside that rectangle and add on the rest of the shapes. Make the circle for Dabura's dastardly right hand extra large. He's going to reach out and grab you!

TAKE THAT!
Dabura can change his enemies into stone, just by spitting on them!

BREAK IT DOWN
Whoa! Check out that hand! Time to practice on a piece of scrap paper. Here's a hint: Figure out size of each finger in Step 2, when you're still drawing basic shapes.

2 Quickly sketch in the outline. Add the face and ears. To make the master of the underworld look like he's leaping down from above, draw Dabura's cape flowing up behind him.

3

Take some extra time to go over the
lines you drew in Step 2. Is everything
in proportion? Look at how much
shorter the right arm is than the left
arm. The left hand is the biggest part
of Dabura's menacing body!

5

It's time to give Dabura
some detail! Erase any
lines you don't need
and darken in Dabura's
hair. Spend some time
working on the draping
of his clothing and the
details in his hands and
face.

4

Now clean it up. Check the proportions one
more time. See how small Dabura's right foot
is compared to his right knee? Use a marker
or dark pencil to go over the outlines.

CHALLENGE ARENA

Dabura thinks Buu is out-of-control
dangerous. Try drawing Dabura challenging Majin Buu to a face-off. Who will
win? Who will be eliminated? Draw the
winner taking on Super Saiyan 3 Goku in
a championship round!

SUPER SAIYAN MAJIN VEGETA®

At long last, Vegeta gets his chance to fight Goku! But to do it, he has to take a walk on the evil side. To gain the extra power he needs, Vegeta surrenders himself to the dangerous powers of Babidi and becomes a bad guy!

1

Does this setup look like anything you've drawn before? The arrangement of shapes in this drawing is similar to that in the drawing of Gotenks. Now go to it!

With light, loose lines and Super Saiyan Majin speed, sketch the outline. Then decide where the hair and face will be.

2

MAJIN MUCH?
Don't forget the M on Super Saiyan Majin Vegeta's forehead. He may never be completely under the control of the evil wizard, Babidi, but that M on Vegeta's forehead shows that he's definitely under Babidi's evil influence.

3 Check the proportions and the shapes. Then clean up your lines. Remember to draw on top of the lines you've already drawn in Steps 1 and 2.

WHEN HE'S BAD . . .
. . . he's bad. But when he's good, he's Super Saiyan good. Never fear! Vegeta doesn't stay Majin for long. When Vegeta fights to save Earth, the M on his forehead disappears. He's even willing to make the ultimate sacrifice for Earth's sake.

Go over the lines you want to keep with a marker or dark pencil. Then erase any lines you don't need. Start adding details to the face and hands. Don't forget to draw Vegeta's powerful boots and the tears in his pants.

4

5 It's time for the finishing touches! Use short, quick lines to show how dirty Vegeta got from fighting. Then take a close look at his arms and forehead — Vegeta is so angry that his veins are popping out!

CHALLENGE ARENA
Now that you can draw Super Saiyan Majin Vegeta and Super Saiyan 3 Goku, it's time to draw the Challenge Arena battle of the century! Vegeta has been waiting his entire life for this face-off. Who will win in your drawing?

BABIDI™

Babidi uses his awesome powers to bring out the evil in people's hearts and then uses it to control them. He even unleashes the destructive power of Buu by breaking the seal on Buu's cocoon. Can you capture the power of Babidi on paper?

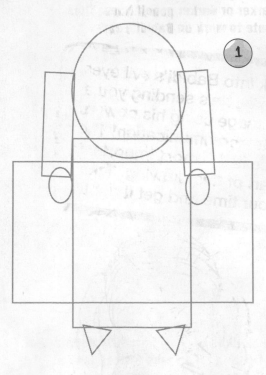

1 The shapes in this drawing are bigger than in other drawings. Start with a big rectangle for the body and a big circle for Babidi's large head. Then add on the rest of the shapes.

2 Use curving lines to quickly transform the shapes into an outline. Set up the face and Babidi's big buglike eyes.

CHANGE IT UP!

When you draw over your final lines in marker or darker pencil, vary the thickness. Make them thicker in the middle and thinner at the ends. Detail lines in the clothes, hair, and textures should taper out to points. Practice draping clothes, shading hair, and creating textures on scrap paper.

③ Clean the lines you drew in Step 2 and go over them in marker or darker pencil lines. Then take a minute to work on Babidi's cape.

Look into Babidi's evil eyes. Maybe he's sending you a message using his powers of telecommunication! The face is the most important part of this drawing. Take your time and get it right.

④ Erase any extra lines and add details. The wrinkles on this dark wizard's head are quick curves. Remember to vary the width and size of your lines. The hairs are thick at the bottom and thin at the top.

CHALLENGE ARENA

Let the battles begin! Redraw this Challenge Arena on a large sheet of paper. Then place two figures in the spotlight for the ultimate face-off. It's time to choose which side you're on. Who will prevail? Good or evil?

STEP IT UP!

Here's a hint to help you recreate your own Challenge Arena. All those vertical lines in the floor meet at the same point. The horizontal lines are all parallel. They will never meet. The stands are just big, sweeping curves. Practice drawing curves on scrap paper before trying your drawing! Of course, you can always start by tracing the arena, just to get the hang of it!

Now that you can draw the amazing DBZ warriors and this awesome stadium background, put it all together. You can create your own Super Saiyan saga. Remember, the fate of the universe is in your hands. And that means the action is up to you!

SAVE THE BEST FOR LAST

Don't even think about adding details like the wrinkles on the hand or the folds in the clothing until you've got the basic outline of the character on your paper. You could end up with a perfect eye on a head that's way too small for the body. Or an excellent hand that's in the wrong place!